Baby's First Five Years

A Baby Record Book

The Land oF MiLk & Honey™

HARVEST HOUSE PUBLISHERS

EUGENE, OREGON

Baby's First Five Years

Text Copyright © 2005 by Harvest House Publishers
Eugene, Oregon 97402

ISBN-10: 0-7369-1543-5
ISBN-13: 978-0-7369-1543-4

The Land of Milk & Honey™ © 2005 by G Studios, LLC. The Land of Milk & Honey Trademarks owned by G Studios, LLC, Newport Beach, CA USA and used by Harvest House Publishers, Inc., under authorization. For more information regarding art featured in this book, please contact:

G Studios, LLC
4500 Campus Drive, Suite 200
Newport Beach, CA 92660
949.261.1300
www.gstudiosllc.com

Design and production by Garborg Design Works, Inc., Minneapolis, Minnesota

Harvest House Publishers has made every effort to trace the ownership of all poems and quotes. In the event of a question arising from the use of a poem or quote, we regret any error made and will be pleased to make the necessary correction in future editions of this book.

Scripture quotations are taken from the Holy Bible, New International Version®, Copyright © 1973, 1978, 1984 by the International Bible Society. Used by permission of Zondervan Publishing House.

Printed in China

05 06 07 08 09 10 11 12 / IM / 10 9 8 7 6 5 4 3 2 1

A new baby is like
the beginning of all
things—wonder,
hope, a dream
of possibilities.

Eda LeShan

This special book belongs to

Your proud parents are

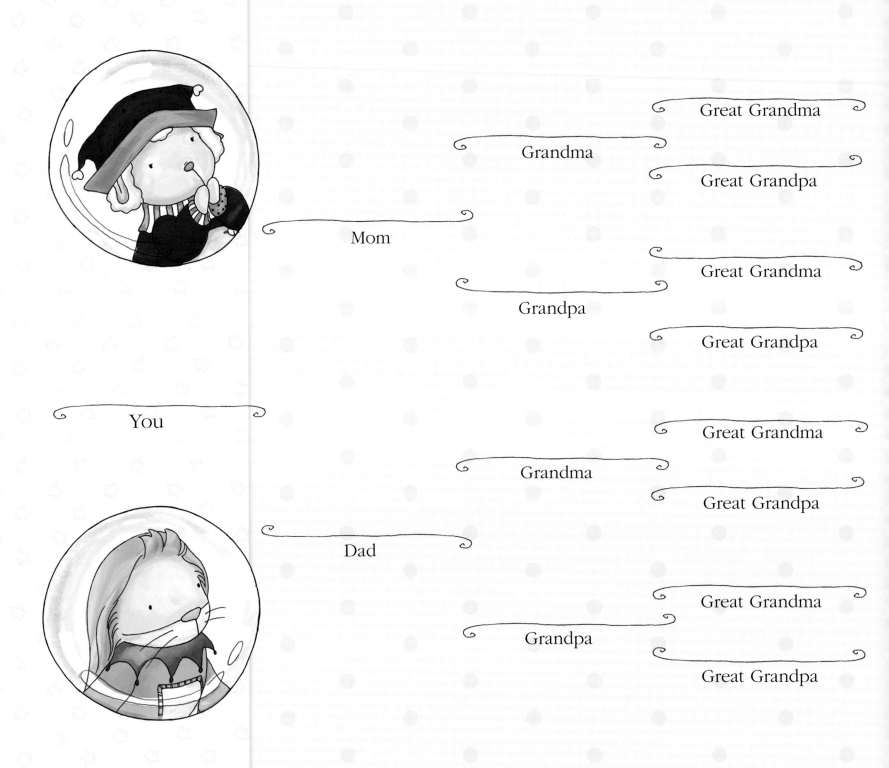

You

Mom

Grandma

Great Grandma

Great Grandpa

Grandpa

Great Grandma

Great Grandpa

Dad

Grandma

Great Grandma

Great Grandpa

Grandpa

Great Grandma

Great Grandpa

Our Family Tree

Your mom was born in: _____

_____

Her family came from: _____

_____

She grew up in: _____

_____

Your dad was born in: _____

_____

His family came from: _____

_____

He grew up in: _____

_____

How Mom and Dad met: _____

_____

_____

When Mom and Dad got married and where: _____

_____

_____

Your Pending Arrival

The day Mom and Dad discovered you were on the way: _____

_____

Mom's first reaction: _____

_____

Dad's first reaction: _____

_____

Your due date was: _____

Your doctor was: _____

The doctor told Mom to: _____

_____

Books Mom and Dad read: _____

_____

Classes they took: _____

_____

Foods Mom couldn't live without: _____

Pregnancy highlights: _____

_____

_____

_____

Welcoming a newborn baby is somehow absolute, truer and more binding than any other experience that life has to offer.

MARILYN FRENCH

You Are Truly Unique

First: _____ Middle: _____ Last: _____

How Mom and Dad chose this name: _____
_____
_____

Your name means: _____
_____

Nicknames people call you: _____
_____

Other names considered

For a boy: For a girl:

_____   _____

_____   _____

_____   _____

Showers of Blessings

(PLACE SHOWER INVITATION HERE.)

Special moments:

_____

_____

_____

_____

Gifts You Received

_____

_____

_____

_____

_____

_____

_____

Children are a
wonderful gift…They
have an extraordinary
capacity to see into
the heart of things.
Desmond Tutu

_____

_____

_____

_____

The Day You Were Born

When and where labor began: _____

_____

_____

_____

Labor and delivery: _____

_____

_____

Hospital where you were born: _____

Who was present at your birth: _____

_____

_____

Special memories: _____

Behold, children
are a gift of
the Lord.

THE BOOK OF PSALMS

_____

_____

_____

_____

Happy Birth Day

You were born on: _____ At: _____

Time: _____ Doctor who delivered you: _____

You weighed: _____ And were this long: _____

Your eyes were: _____ Your hair was: _____

You looked most like: _____

_____

_____

(PLACE FIRST PHOTO HERE.)

There was a star danced, and under that I was born.

WILLIAM SHAKESPEARE

What in the World Was Going On the Day You Were Born...

Major world events: _____

The president: _____

Favorite TV shows: _____

Stars: _____

Hit songs: _____

Big movies: _____

A gallon of milk cost: _____

A loaf of bread cost: _____

(PLACE NEWSPAPER CLIPPINGS HERE.)

(PLACE POSTAGE STAMP HERE.)

A baby is God's opinion that the world should go on.

Carl Sandburg

Your First Imprints

Left Hand   Right Hand

Left Foot   Right Foot

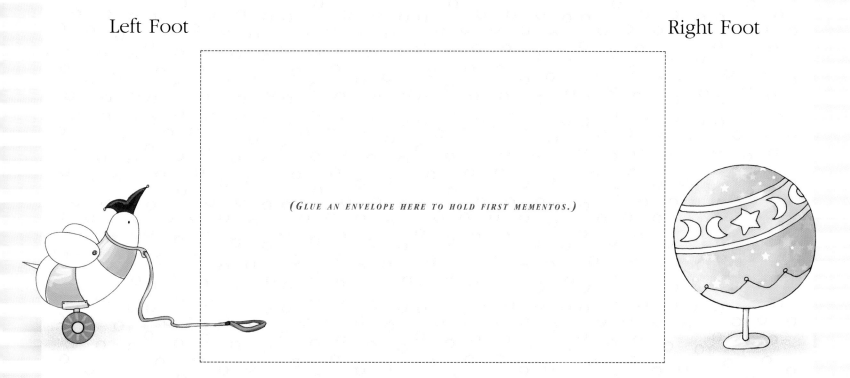

(GLUE AN ENVELOPE HERE TO HOLD FIRST MEMENTOS.)

Here's Baby!

(Place baby announcement here.)

Welcome to Our World

People who came to welcome you: _____
_____
_____
_____

Messages from family: _____
_____
_____
_____

Messages from friends: _____
_____
_____
_____

For You have formed my inward parts;
You have covered me in my mother's womb.
I will praise You, for I am
fearfully and wonderfully made...

The Book of Psalms

Home Sweet Home

You came home to: _____
(address)

On: _____
(day & date)

Your nursery was decorated with: _____

_____

_____

_____

Your first night home you: _____

_____

_____

_____

_____

(PICTURE OF YOU IN YOUR ROOM.)

Your First Bathtime Adventure

_____

_____

_____

_____

_____

_____

(PLACE PHOTO HERE.)

All By Myself

Slept through the night: _____

_____

Went on my first outing: _____

_____

Discovered my hands and feet: _____

_____

Smiled: _____

_____

Sat up by myself: _____

_____

Rolled over: _____

_____

Giggled: _____

_____

Stood up alone: _____

Spoke my first word: _____

_____

Crawled: _____

_____

Toddled my first steps: _____

_____

Cut my first tooth: _____

_____

Waved bye-bye: _____

_____

Called Mom or Dad by name: _____

_____

Played peek-a-boo: _____

_____

Blew a kiss: _____

_____

Fed myself: _____

Dressed myself: _____

_____

Rode my tricycle: _____

_____

Tied my shoes: _____

_____

There is one order of beauty which seems
made to turn heads…It is a beauty like that
of kittens, or very small downy ducks
making gentle rippling noises with their soft
bills, or babies just beginning to toddle…

George Eliot

Religious Celebration

Our place of worship: _____

Type of ceremony: _____

_____

_____

Date: _____

Who was there: _____

_____

_____

Special prayers: _____

_____

_____

_____

Thoughts about this day: _____

_____

_____

_____

Train a child in the way he should go, and when he is old he will not turn from it.

THE BOOK OF PROVERBS

I'm Sooooo Big!

(PLACE PHOTO HERE.)

First Month

height: _____

weight: _____

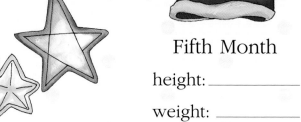

Fifth Month

height: _____

weight: _____

Second Month

height: _____

weight: _____

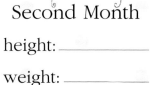

Fourth Month

height: _____

weight: _____

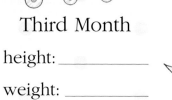

Third Month

height: _____

weight: _____

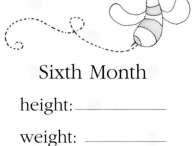

Sixth Month

height: _____

weight: _____

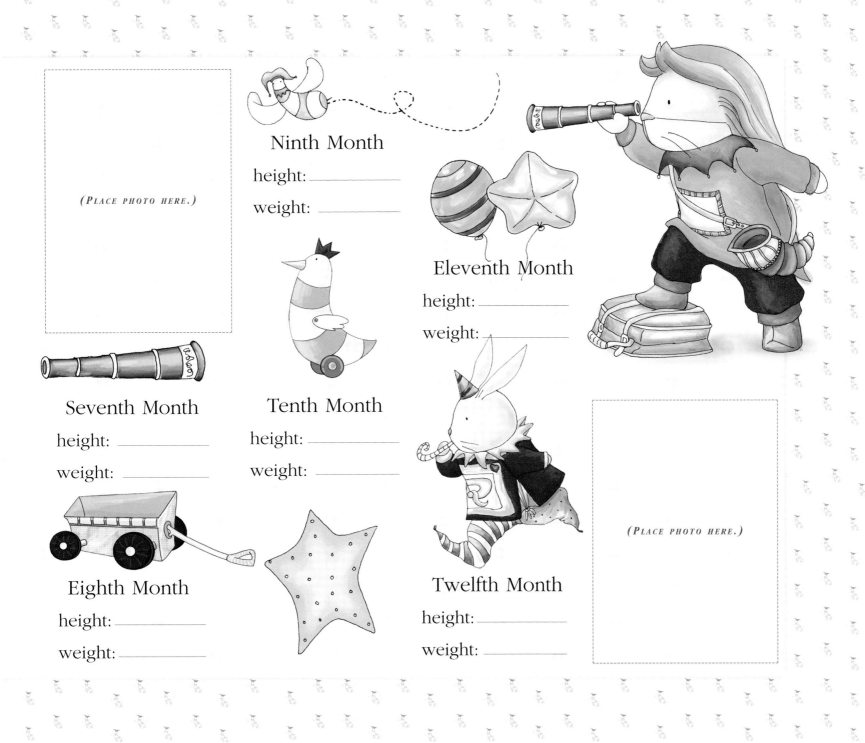

Ninth Month

height: _____

weight: _____

Eleventh Month

height: _____

weight: _____

(PLACE PHOTO HERE.)

Seventh Month

height: _____

weight: _____

Tenth Month

height: _____

weight: _____

Eighth Month

height: _____

weight: _____

Twelfth Month

height: _____

weight: _____

(PLACE PHOTO HERE.)

First Christmas Keepsakes

Special memories: _____

_____

_____

_____

(PLACE PHOTO HERE.)

What was in your first stocking: _____

_____

People who celebrated with us: _____

_____

Favorite presents: _____

_____

Family traditions: _____

_____

_____

Sleep well, little children, pleasant dreams through the night;
Tomorrow is Christmas all merry and bright.
Soon you'll hear the bells ring, time for dreams to come true
As the world wakes to bring Merry Christmas to you.

A. BERGMAN AND L. KLATZKIN

Other Holiday Celebrations

(PLACE PHOTO HERE.)

Memorable moments:

_____

_____

_____

_____

_____

_____

_____

_____

_____

_____

(PLACE PHOTO HERE.)

(PLACE PHOTO HERE.)

Your First Birthday

How we celebrated: _____

_____

_____

Guests and gifts: _____

_____

_____

Memorable moments: _____

_____

_____

_____

_____

_____

_____

(PLACE PHOTO HERE.)

(Place photo here.)

(Place photo here.)

Your Second Birthday

How we celebrated: _____

_____

_____

Guests and gifts: _____

_____

_____

Memorable moments: _____

_____

_____

_____

_____

_____

_____

_____

(PLACE PHOTO HERE.)

(PLACE PHOTO HERE.)

(PLACE PHOTO HERE.)

Your Terrific (and Not So Terrific) Twos

How Mom and Dad survived: _____

_____

_____

You were a handful because: _____

_____

_____

You "helped" Mom by: _____

_____

_____

You could do this all by yourself: _____

_____

_____

_____

A Few of Your Favorite Things

Games: _____

_____

Toys: _____

_____

Activities: _____

_____

Songs: _____

_____

Stories: _____

_____

Animals: _____

_____

Blankie: _____

_____

Children make a special kind
of sense all their own.

Art Linkletter

Your Favorite Foods

Your favorite foods and snacks: _____

_____

_____

Foods you were not so fond of: _____

_____

_____

(PLACE PHOTO HERE.)

Your Favorite Childhood Pals

Name: _____

Memories: _____

_____

_____

_____

_____

Name: _____

Memories: _____

_____

_____

_____

_____

Name: _____

Memories: _____

_____

_____

_____

_____

God made the world so broad and so grand,
Filled with blessings from His hand.
He made the sky so high and blue,
And all the little children, too.

Author Unknown

Your Adventures Through the Seasons

(PICTURES OF YOU IN SUMMER.)

(PICTURES OF YOU IN FALL.)

(PICTURES OF YOU IN WINTER.)

(PICTURES OF YOU IN SPRING.)

Your Third Birthday

How we celebrated: _____
_____
_____

Guests and gifts: _____
_____
_____

Memorable moments: _____
_____
_____
_____
_____
_____
_____

(PLACE PHOTO HERE.)

(PLACE PHOTO HERE.)

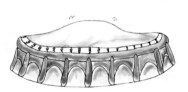

(PLACE PHOTO HERE.)

Your First Day of Preschool

Date: _____   At: _____

Your teacher was: _____

Your favorite thing about preschool was: _____

_____

_____

_____

Memorable moments: _____

_____

_____

_____

You are Special

_____

_____

_____

(PLACE PHOTO HERE.)

Your favorite songs and games were: _____

_____

_____

_____

_____

_____

_____

From small beginnings
come great things.

Author Unknown

Your First Haircut

You had your first haircut on:_____

_____

Who cut your hair: _____

_____

_____

(PLACE ENVELOPE HERE THAT
INCLUDES A LOCK OF HAIR.)

Lost Teeth and Toothless Grins

You lost your first tooth: _____

_____

The tooth fairy left you: _____

_____

_____

_____

(PLACE PICTURE HERE
OF TOOTHLESS GRIN.)

Adventures with Art

(GLUE OR PASTE PICTURE HERE, AGE:)

Your Fourth Birthday

How we celebrated: _____
_____
_____

Guests and gifts: _____
_____
_____

Memorable moments: _____
_____
_____
_____

(PLACE PHOTO HERE.)

Children are likely to live up
to what you believe of them.

Ladybird Johnson

(PLACE PHOTO HERE.)

(PLACE PHOTO HERE.)

Your Fifth Birthday

How we celebrated: _____

_____

_____

Guests and gifts: _____

_____

_____

Memorable moments: _____

_____

_____

_____

_____

_____

_____

_____

_____

(PLACE PHOTO HERE.)

(Place photo here.)

(Place photo here.)

Your First Day of Kindergarten

Your first day of school was: _____ At: _____

Your teacher was: _____

Your new friends were: _____

_____

_____

Your favorite part of school was: _____

_____

You learned how to: _____

_____

Memorable moments: _____

_____

_____

_____

_____

_____

Children are made of eyes and ears, and nothing, however minute, escapes their microscopic observation.

Fanny Kemble

(Place kindergarten photo here.)

Hopes and Dreams for the Future

What feeling is so nice as
a child's hand in yours?

Marjorie Holmes

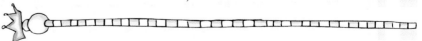

Some Thoughts from Mom and Dad on the First Five Years

Mom: _____

_____

_____

_____

_____

_____

_____

_____

_____

_____

Dad: _____

_____

_____

_____

_____

_____

_____

_____

_____

_____